EXPLORING OUR OCEANS

SOUTHERN OCEAN

by Avery Toolen

pogo

Ideas for Parents and Teachers

Pogo Books let children practice reading informational text while introducing them to nonfiction features such as headings, labels, sidebars, maps, and diagrams, as well as a table of contents, glossary, and index.

Carefully leveled text with a strong photo match offers early fluent readers the support they need to succeed.

Before Reading

- "Walk" through the book and point out the various nonfiction features. Ask the student what purpose each feature serves.
- Look at the glossary together. Read and discuss the words.

Read the Book

- Have the child read the book independently.
- Invite him or her to list questions that arise from reading.

After Reading

- Discuss the child's questions. Talk about how he or she might find answers to those questions.
- Prompt the child to think more. Ask: Many ships have sunk in the Southern Ocean. Why do you think this is?

Pogo Books are published by Jump!
5357 Penn Avenue South
Minneapolis, MN 55419
www.jumplibrary.com

Library of Congress Cataloging-in-Publication Data

Names: Toolen, Avery, author.
Title: Southern Ocean / by Avery Toolen.
Description: Minneapolis, MN: Jump!, Inc., 2023.
Series: Exploring our oceans | Includes index.
Audience: Ages 7-10
Identifiers: LCCN 2021054983 (print)
LCCN 2021054984 (ebook)
ISBN 9781636907802 (hardcover)
ISBN 9781636907826 (paperback)
ISBN 9781636907819 (ebook)
Subjects: LCSH: Antarctic Ocean–Juvenile literature.
Marine ecology–Antarctic Ocean–Juvenile literature.
Classification: LCC GC461 .T66 2023 (print)
LCC GC461 (ebook)
DDC 910.9167–dc23
LC record available at
https://lccn.loc.gov/2021054983
LC ebook record available at
https://lccn.loc.gov/2021054984

Editor: Jenna Gleisner
Designer: Emma Bersie

Photo Credits: Jan Martin Will/Shutterstock, cover (penguins); Peter Kaple/Shutterstock, cover (seal); Philip Schubert/Shutterstock, 1; Christian Weber/Shutterstock, 3; Steve Allen/Shutterstock, 4; Amelie Koch/Shutterstock, 5; Naeblys/Shutterstock, 6–7; Manfred Thurig/Alamy, 8–9; tonyzhao120/Shutterstock, 10; Tarpan/Shutterstock, 11; Viktorialvanets/Shutterstock, 12–13 (top); Nick Pecker/Shutterstock, 12–13 (bottom); Ethan Daniels/Shutterstock, 14–15; Bkamprath/iStock, 16; IanDagnall Computing/Alamy, 17; polarman/Shutterstock, 18–19; Eleanor Scriven/Shutterstock, 20–21; Shchipkova Elena/Shutterstock, 23.

Printed in the United States of America at Corporate Graphics in North Mankato, Minnesota.

TABLE OF CONTENTS

CHAPTER 1

ICY OCEAN

What ocean surrounds Antarctica? It is the Southern Ocean! It is also known as the Antarctic Ocean. It is made up of salt water.

This ocean is very cold. Its **average** temperature is between 28 and 50 degrees Fahrenheit (–2 and 10 degrees Celsius). In winter, ice sheets cover parts of this ocean.

Earth's four other oceans are defined by the **continents** that separate them. But no continents separate the Southern Ocean from the others. It touches parts of the Atlantic, Indian, and Pacific Oceans.

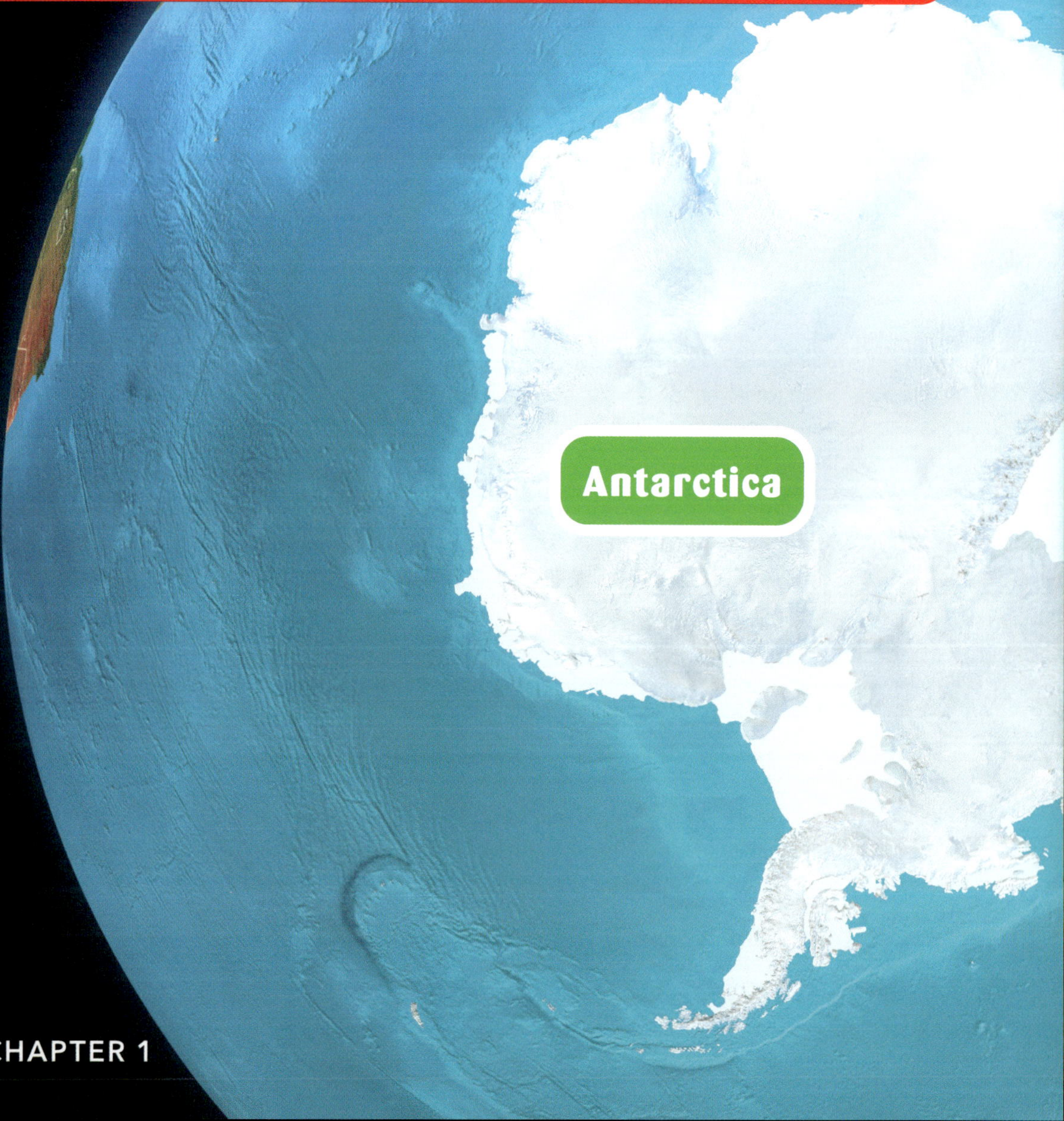

TAKE A LOOK!

Where is the Southern Ocean? Take a look!

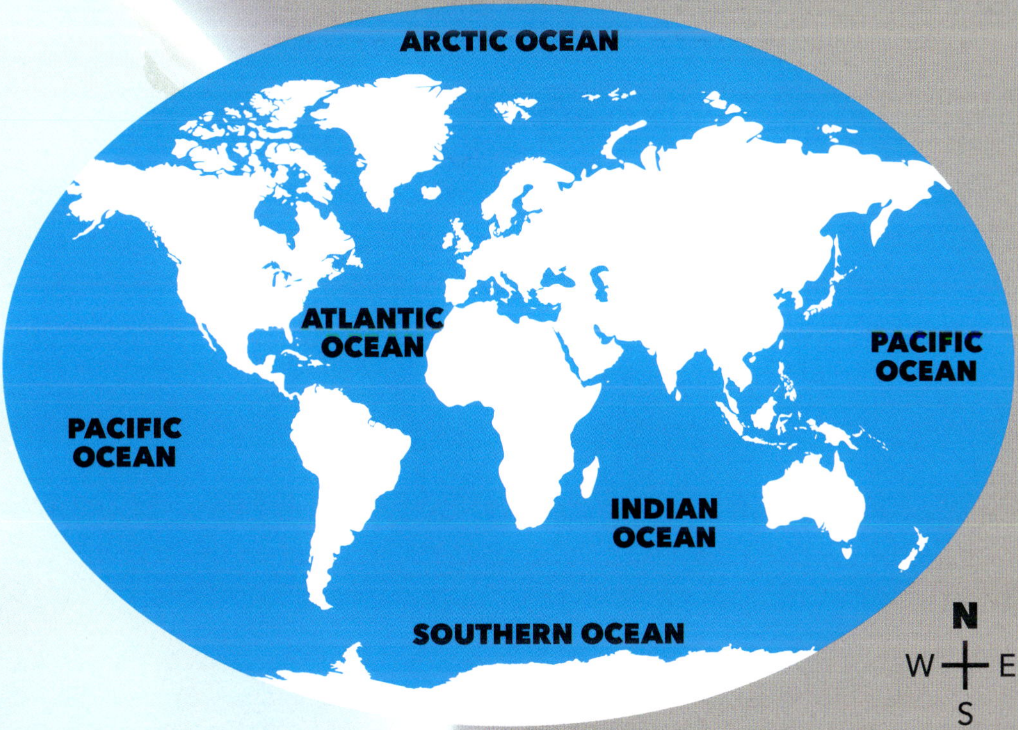

Storms are common in this ocean. They cause high winds. This makes it hard for ships to sail. **Icebergs** also make sailing dangerous.

DID YOU KNOW?

Icebergs break off of **glaciers**. Glaciers are melting due to **climate change**. This causes the **sea level** to rise.

iceberg

CHAPTER 2

LIFE IN THE SOUTHERN OCEAN

Many animals live in the Southern Ocean. Adélie and emperor penguins nest on the ice.

Weddell seals give birth to **pups** on ice. They eat fish and squid. These seals can weigh 1,200 pounds (544 kilograms)!

Birds nest on the shores. Skuas lay eggs in rocky areas. They steal eggs and chicks from Adélie penguin nests.

Albatrosses follow fishing boats. They eat fish parts that are thrown over.

DID YOU KNOW?

Kelp grows in the Southern Ocean. It provides a **habitat** for animals like sea stars and sea urchins.

skua

albatross

Krill are an important part of the ocean's **food web**. Humpback whales, leopard seals, and squid are just a few Antarctic animals that eat krill. Krill eat plankton. These are tiny plants and animals that float in the ocean.

TAKE A LOOK!

Krill are a key part of the Southern Ocean's food web. Take a look!

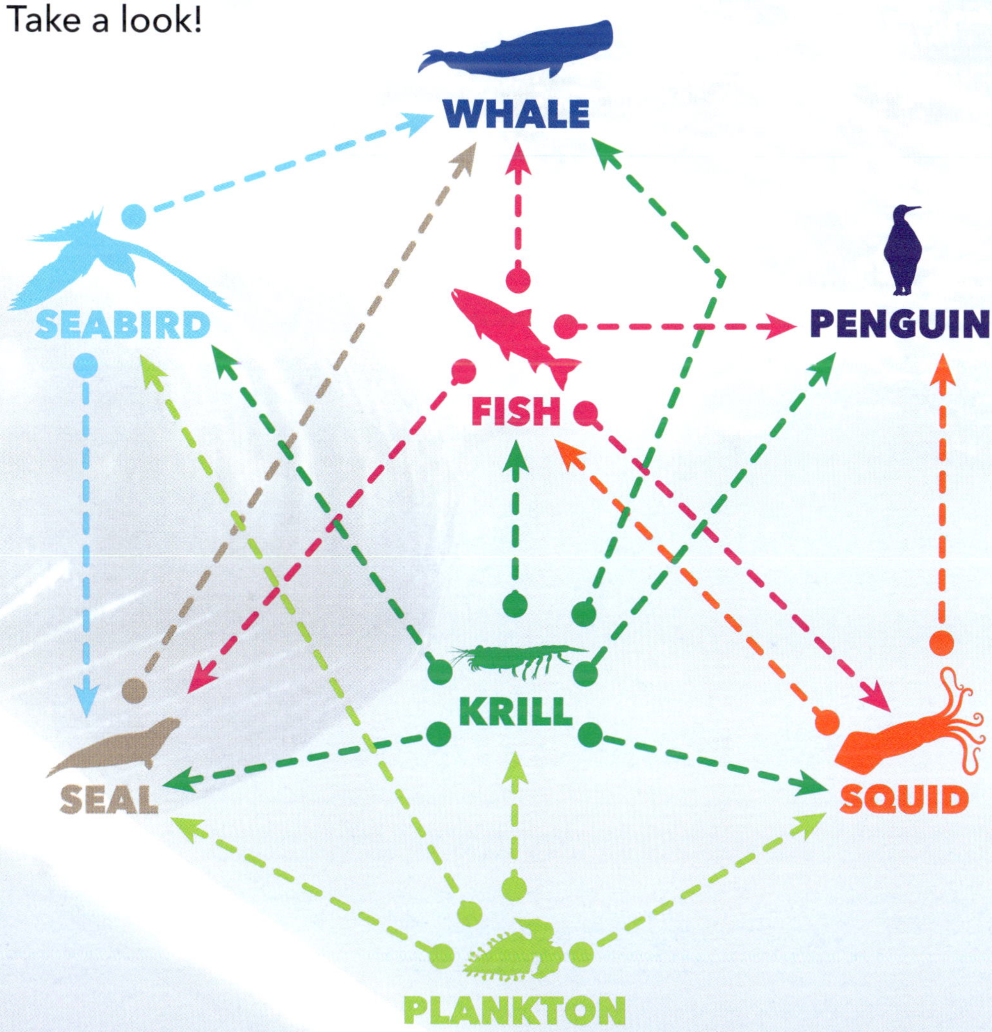

CHAPTER 3

EXPLORING AMONG ICE

People have been exploring the Southern Ocean for hundreds of years. Ice and storms have caused many ships to sink. The *Governoren* was a **whaling ship**. It sank in 1915. We can still see its remains.

That same year, the H.M.S. *Endurance* got stuck in ice. It eventually sank. Ernest Shackleton was the captain. He and the others on the ship sailed a lifeboat 800 miles (1,287 kilometers) to get help. Everyone survived.

H.M.S. *Endurance*

Today, scientists travel here. They sail on big ships that cut through the ice. They map the ocean floor. Underwater cameras and microphones help them learn about ocean animals and plants. Some crews search for sunken ships.

DID YOU KNOW?

Some ships send robots underwater. Why? The ice makes many parts of the ocean hard to get to. Robots can reach areas ships can't.

Tourists explore by boat, too. Some paddle kayaks. Others sail on cruise ships. Would you like to explore the Southern Ocean?

kayak

ACTIVITIES & TOOLS

TRY THIS!

ACT OUT A FOOD WEB

Many food chains make up a food web. See how it works with this fun activity!

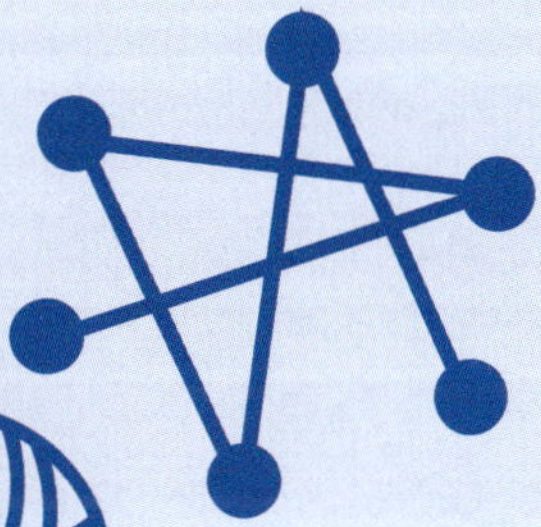

What You Need:

- several classmates or friends
- paper
- colored pencils, markers, or crayons
- tape
- a ball of yarn or string
- scissors

1. **Gather several friends or classmates. Have each person pick a different plant or animal that is part of the Southern Ocean food web.**
2. **Have each person draw their plant or animal and tape it to the front of their shirt.**
3. **Have everyone stand in a big circle. Give the ball of yarn or string to someone who is a plant, such as plankton. This person will hold onto the end of the yarn and throw the ball to an animal that eats it.**
4. **Continue this pattern until the ball reaches an animal at the top of the food chain. Cut the yarn. Start over again and make a new food chain.**
5. **Discuss the activity with the group. How are the food chains connected? How do they make up a food web? What would happen if one part of the web was gone?**

GLOSSARY

average: A number you get by adding a group of numbers together and then dividing the sum by the number of figures you added.

climate change: Changes in Earth's weather and climate over time.

continents: The seven large landmasses on Earth.

food web: The complex network of related food chains within an ecosystem.

glaciers: Slow-moving masses of ice found in mountain valleys or polar regions.

habitat: A place where certain animals or plants are usually found.

icebergs: Large masses of ice that break off from glaciers and float in the sea.

kelp: A type of large brown seaweed.

krill: Small floating sea animals that look like shrimp.

pups: Young seals.

sea level: The average level of the ocean's surface.

tourists: People who travel and visit places for pleasure.

whaling ship: A ship used for hunting whales.

INDEX

TO LEARN MORE

Finding more information is as easy as 1, 2, 3.

1. Go to www.factsurfer.com
2. Enter "SouthernOcean" into the search box.
3. Choose your book to see a list of websites.

FACT SURFER